Introduction

Eating healthy can be a challenge, especially when you're short on time or ideas for what to cook. That's where this book comes in. This cookbook is designed to make healthy eating easy and delicious, with 69 easy-to-follow recipes that are packed with nutrients and low in carbohydrates. Whether you're looking to lose weight, manage diabetes, or simply eat healthier, this book has something for everyone.

benefits of having a healthy food meals:

Eating a healthy diet can have a significant impact on your overall health and well-being. By choosing nutrient-rich foods and avoiding processed and high-calorie foods, you can improve your physical health, mental health, and quality of life. Here are some of the key benefits of eating a healthy diet:

Weight management: A healthy diet can help you maintain a healthy weight or lose weight if you need to. By choosing foods that are low in calories and high in nutrients, you can feel satisfied and full without consuming too many calories.

Reduced risk of chronic diseases: Eating a healthy diet can lower your risk of chronic diseases such as heart disease, stroke, type 2 diabetes, and certain cancers. This is because a healthy diet can help you maintain healthy blood pressure, cholesterol, and blood sugar levels.

Improved mood and mental health: Studies have shown that eating a healthy diet can improve your mood and reduce symptoms of depression and anxiety. This may be because nutrient-rich foods provide the vitamins and minerals your brain needs to function properly.

Increased energy levels: Eating a healthy diet can give you more energy throughout the day. Nutrient-rich foods provide the fuel your body needs to function at its best.

Better sleep: Eating a healthy diet can help you sleep better at night. This is because a healthy diet can regulate your hormones and keep your blood sugar levels stable, which can help you fall asleep faster and stay asleep longer.

Stronger immune system: A healthy diet can boost your immune system and help you fight off infections and diseases. Nutrient-rich foods provide the vitamins and minerals your body needs to produce immune cells and fight off harmful pathogens.

Overall, eating a healthy diet can have a profound impact on your physical and mental health. By choosing nutrient-rich foods and avoiding processed and high-calorie foods, you can improve your overall quality of life and reduce your risk of chronic diseases. So why not start today? Incorporate some of the delicious, healthy recipes from this book into your diet and start reaping the benefits!

tips and tricks to help control your eating habits

Plan your meals: One of the most effective ways to control your eating habits is to plan your meals in advance. By planning out your meals for the week, you can ensure that you have healthy and nutritious foods on hand and avoid impulse eating.

Practice portion control: Eating too much of even healthy foods can lead to weight gain. Use smaller plates and measuring cups to control your portion sizes and avoid overeating.

Eat slowly: Eating too quickly can lead to overeating and indigestion. Take your time when eating and savor each bite. This can help you feel more satisfied with smaller portions.

Choose nutrient dense foods: Nutrient dense foods, such as fruits, vegetables, lean proteins, and whole grains, can provide your body with the vitamins and minerals it needs to function at its best. Aim to include a variety of nutrient dense foods in your diet.

Avoid processed foods: Processed foods are often high in calories, sugar, and unhealthy fats. Try to limit your intake of processed foods and focus on whole, natural foods instead.

Stay hydrated: Drinking plenty of water can help you feel full and avoid overeating. Aim to drink at least eight glasses of water a day.

Listen to your body: Pay attention to your body's hunger and fullness cues. Stop eating when you're full and avoid eating out of boredom or emotions.

By incorporating these tips and tricks into your daily routine, you can take control of your eating habits and improve your overall health and well-being. And with the delicious and nutritious recipes in this book healthy eating has never been easier or more enjoyable!

With "Delicious HEALTHY FOOD 69 EASY LOW CARB MEALS," you can start making positive changes to your diet and lifestyle today. By incorporating the delicious and nutritious recipes in this book into your daily routine, you can improve your overall health and well being and start feeling your best.

Whether you're looking to lose weight, manage a chronic condition, or simply eat healthier, this book has something for everyone. With 69 easy to follow recipes that are low in carbs and high in nutrients, you'll be able to enjoy delicious and satisfying meals that will keep you energized and nourished throughout the day.

So why wait? Start reading "Delicious HEALTHY FOOD 69 EASY LOW CARB MEALS" today and take the first step towards a healthier and happier lifestyle. Whether you're a seasoned cook or a beginner in the kitchen, these recipes are easy to follow and will help you create delicious meals that you and your family will love. Get ready to transform your diet and start feeling your best!

Enjoy your meals..

Garlic Butter
Steak Bites

Ingredients

1 lb. sirloin steak, trimmed and cut into small bite-sized pieces

2 tablespoons butter

2 cloves garlic, minced

Salt and pepper, to taste

Fresh parsley, chopped (optional)

Directions

1. Preheat a large skillet over high heat.
2. Pat the steak bites dry with a paper towel and season them generously with salt and pepper.
3. Add 1 tablespoon of butter to the skillet and let it melt.
4. Add the steak bites to the skillet and cook for 2-3 minutes on each side until browned and cooked to your desired level of doneness.
5. Remove the steak bites from the skillet and set them aside on a plate.
6. In the same skillet, add the remaining tablespoon of butter and the minced garlic. Cook the garlic for 1-2 minutes, until fragrant.
7. Return the steak bites to the skillet and toss them in the garlic butter until they are coated.
8. Remove the skillet from the heat and transfer the steak bites to a serving dish.
9. Garnish with chopped parsley (optional) and serve immediately.

CAULIFLOWER
FRIED RICE

Ingredients:

- 1 head cauliflower, chopped into florets
- 1 tablespoon olive oil
- 1/2 cup diced onion
- 1/2 cup diced carrots
- 1/2 cup frozen peas
- 2 cloves garlic, minced
- 2 eggs, lightly beaten
- 3 tablespoons soy sauce
- Salt and pepper, to taste
- Green onions, sliced (optional)

Instructions:

1. Place the cauliflower florets in a food processor and pulse until they resemble small grains of rice.
2. Heat a large skillet over medium heat and add the olive oil.
3. Add the onions and carrots to the skillet and cook for 3-4 minutes until they are soft.
4. Add the cauliflower rice and frozen peas to the skillet and cook for 3-4 minutes until the cauliflower is tender.
5. Add the garlic to the skillet and cook for an additional minute until fragrant.
6. Push the rice mixture to one side of the skillet and add the beaten eggs to the other side. Scramble the eggs until they are cooked through.
7. Mix the scrambled eggs into the rice mixture and add soy sauce. Toss everything together until it's well combined.
8. Season with salt and pepper to taste.
9. Garnish with sliced green onions, if desired, and serve immediately.

ZUCCHINI NOODLES WITH PESTO

INGREDIENTS

4 medium zucchini,
spiralized

1/2 cup basil leaves

1/4 cup pine nuts

1/4 cup grated
Parmesan cheese

1/4 cup olive oil

2 cloves garlic, minced

Salt and pepper, to
taste

Cherry tomatoes, sliced
(optional)

DIRECTIONS

1. Spiralize the zucchini into noodles using a spiralizer.
2. In a food processor, combine the basil, pine nuts,
   Parmesan cheese, olive oil, garlic, salt, and pepper.
   Pulse until the mixture forms a paste.
3. Heat a large skillet over medium heat.
4. Add the pesto to the skillet and cook for 1-2 minutes
   until fragrant.
5. Add the zucchini noodles to the skillet and toss them
   in the pesto until they are well coated. Cook for 2-3
   minutes until the zucchini noodles are tender but
   still firm.
6. Remove the skillet from heat and transfer the
   zucchini noodles to a serving dish.
7. Top with sliced cherry tomatoes, if desired.
8. Serve immediately and enjoy your healthy and
   delicious zucchini noodles with pesto!

Keto Shrimp Scampi

Ingredients

1 lb. shrimp, peeled and
deveined
2 tablespoons butter
2 tablespoons olive oil
3 cloves garlic, minced
1/4 teaspoon red pepper flakes
1/4 cup chicken broth
1/4 cup dry white wine
2 tablespoons lemon juice
2 tablespoons chopped parsley
Salt and pepper, to taste
Zucchini noodles or
cauliflower rice, for serving

Method

1. Heat a large skillet over medium heat.
2. Add the butter and olive oil to the skillet and let the
   butter melt.
3. Add the shrimp to the skillet and cook for 2-3 minutes
   on each side until pink and cooked through. Remove
   the shrimp from the skillet and set them aside on a
   plate.
4. In the same skillet, add the garlic and red pepper flakes.
   Cook for 1-2 minutes until fragrant.
5. Add the chicken broth, white wine, and lemon juice to
   the skillet. Bring the mixture to a simmer and cook for
   2-3 minutes until the liquid has reduced by half.
6. Return the shrimp to the skillet and toss them in the
   sauce until they are well coated.
7. Stir in the chopped parsley and season with salt and
   pepper to taste.
8. Serve the shrimp scampi over zucchini noodles or
   cauliflower rice.

Broccoli Cheese
Soup

Ingredients

4 cups broccoli florets

2 tablespoons butter

1/2 cup diced onion

2 cloves garlic, minced

3 cups chicken broth

1 cup heavy cream

2 cups shredded cheddar cheese

Salt and pepper, to taste

Directions

1. In a large pot, melt the butter over medium heat.

2. Add the onions and garlic to the pot and cook for 2-3 minutes until softened.

3. Add the broccoli florets and chicken broth to the pot. Bring to a boil and then reduce the heat to a simmer. Cook for 10-15 minutes until the broccoli is tender.

4. Using an immersion blender or a regular blender, puree the soup until it's smooth and creamy.

5. Stir in the heavy cream and shredded cheddar cheese until the cheese is melted and the soup is well combined.

6. Season with salt and pepper to taste.

7. Serve the soup hot and garnish with additional shredded cheddar cheese and broccoli florets, if desired.

8. Enjoy your creamy and delicious Broccoli Cheese Soup!

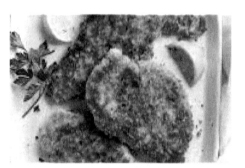

PARMESAN CRUSTED CHICKEN

Ingredients:

- 4 boneless, skinless chicken breasts
- 1 cup grated Parmesan cheese
- 1 cup almond flour
- 2 teaspoons garlic powder
- 2 teaspoons dried oregano
- 2 teaspoons paprika
- 1 teaspoon salt
- 1/2 teaspoon black pepper
- 2 eggs, beaten
- 1/4 cup olive oil

Instructions:

1. Preheat the oven to 400°F.
2. In a shallow dish, combine the Parmesan cheese, almond flour, garlic powder, oregano, paprika, salt, and black pepper
3. In another shallow dish, beat the eggs.
4. Dip each chicken breast in the beaten eggs and then coat it in the Parmesan mixture, pressing the mixture onto the chicken to ensure it sticks.
5. Heat the olive oil in a large skillet over medium heat.
6. Once the oil is hot, add the chicken breasts to the skillet and cook for 2-3 minutes on each side until browned.
7. Transfer the chicken breasts to a baking sheet and bake in the oven for 15-20 minutes until the chicken is cooked through and the Parmesan crust is golden brown
8. Serve the Parmesan Crusted Chicken hot with your favorite sides.

CREAMY GARLIC MUSHROOMS

INGREDIENTS

2 tbsp butter
1 tbsp olive oil
1 lb mushrooms, sliced
3 cloves garlic, minced
1/2 cup heavy cream
1/4 cup grated
Parmesan cheese
Salt and pepper to taste

DIRECTIONS

1. Heat the butter and olive oil in a large skillet over medium-high heat.
2. Add the mushrooms and cook until they release their moisture and start to brown, about 5-7 minutes.
3. Add the garlic and cook for another minute.
4. Add the heavy cream and Parmesan cheese, and stir until the cheese is melted and the sauce is creamy.
5. Season with salt and pepper to taste.
6. Serve hot as a side dish or over pasta.

Bacon and Cheese Stuffed Peppers

Ingredients

4 large bell peppers, halved
and seeded
1 lb ground beef
6 slices bacon, cooked and
crumbled
1 cup shredded cheddar cheese
1/2 cup diced onion
1/2 cup diced tomatoes
2 cloves garlic, minced
Salt and pepper to taste

Method

1. Preheat oven to 375°F
2. In a large skillet, cook the ground beef over medium
heat until browned and no longer pink.
3. Add the bacon, onion, tomatoes, garlic, salt, and
pepper to the skillet and stir to combine.
4. Stuff each pepper half with the beef mixture and
place on a baking sheet
5. Top each pepper with shredded cheddar cheese
6. Bake for 25-30 minutes, or until the peppers are
tender and the cheese is melted and bubbly
7. enjoy

Lemon Garlic Butter Chicken Thighs

Ingredients

4 chicken thighs, bone-in and skin-on

Salt and pepper to taste

2 tbsp butter

2 cloves garlic, minced

1/2 cup chicken broth

Juice of 1 lemon

1 tbsp chopped fresh parsley

Directions

1. Preheat oven to 400°F.

2. Season the chicken thighs with salt and pepper.

3. Heat the butter in a large oven-safe skillet over medium-high heat.

4. Add the chicken thighs, skin-side down, and cook for 5-7 minutes, or until browned and crispy.

5. Flip the chicken thighs and add the garlic to the skillet. Cook for another minute.

6. Pour in the chicken broth and lemon juice and stir to combine.

7. Transfer the skillet to the preheated oven and bake for 25-30 minutes, or until the chicken is cooked through.

8. Remove from oven and sprinkle with chopped parsley before serving.

GREEK SALAD WITH FETA AND OLIVES

Ingredients:

- 2 cups of romaine lettuce, chopped
- 1/2 cup of cherry tomatoes, halved
- 1/2 cup of cucumber, chopped
- 1/4 cup of red onion, thinly sliced
- 1/4 cup of Kalamata olives
- 1/4 cup of crumbled feta cheese
- 2 tablespoons of extra-virgin olive oil
- 1 tablespoon of red wine vinegar
- 1 teaspoon of dried oregano
- Salt and black pepper to taste

Procedure:

1. In a large bowl, add the chopped romaine lettuce, cherry tomatoes, cucumber, and sliced red onion.
2. Top with Kalamata olives and crumbled feta cheese.
3. In a small bowl, whisk together the olive oil, red wine vinegar, dried oregano, salt, and black pepper to make the dressing.
4. Pour the dressing over the salad and toss to combine.
5. Serve and enjoy!

SPINACH AND ARTICHOKE STUFFED CHICKEN

INGREDIENTS

4 boneless, skinless chicken breasts

1/2 cup chopped spinach

1/2 cup chopped artichoke hearts

1/2 cup cream cheese, softened

1/2 cup shredded mozzarella cheese

1/4 cup grated parmesan cheese

1 teaspoon garlic powder

Salt and pepper to taste

Olive oil

DIRECTIONS

1. Preheat oven to 375°F (190°C).
2. In a mixing bowl, combine spinach, artichoke hearts, cream cheese, mozzarella cheese, parmesan cheese, garlic powder, salt, and pepper. Mix well.
3. Lay the chicken breasts flat on a cutting board and make a horizontal slit along the side of each one to create a pocket.
4. Stuff the spinach and artichoke mixture into each pocket, using a toothpick to secure the opening.
5. Heat olive oil in a large skillet over medium-high heat. Sear the stuffed chicken breasts for 2-3 minutes on each side until browned.
6. Transfer the chicken to a baking dish and bake in the oven for 20-25 minutes or until the internal temperature reaches 165°F (74°C).
7. Serve hot and enjoy your low-carb Spinach and Artichoke Stuffed Chicken!

Low-Carb Bolognese with Zucchini Noodles

Ingredients

4 medium-sized zucchinis, spiralized into noodles
1 pound ground beef
1/2 onion, diced
2 cloves garlic, minced
1 can (14.5 ounces) diced tomatoes
1 can (6 ounces) tomato paste
1 tablespoon olive oil
1 tablespoon Italian seasoning
Salt and pepper to taste
Parmesan cheese, grated (optional)

Method

1. In a large skillet, heat olive oil over medium-high heat. Add onion and garlic, sauté until onion is translucent.
2. Add ground beef, break up with a spoon, and cook until browned.
3. Add diced tomatoes, tomato paste, Italian seasoning, salt, and pepper. Stir to combine.
4. Bring mixture to a boil, then reduce heat and simmer for 15-20 minutes or until sauce has thickened.
5. In another skillet, heat olive oil over medium-high heat. Add zucchini noodles and sauté for 2-3 minutes or until tender.
6. Serve zucchini noodles topped with bolognese sauce. Sprinkle with grated Parmesan cheese if desired.
7. Enjoy your delicious low-carb meal!

Buffalo Chicken
Lettuce Wraps

Ingredients

1 pound boneless, skinless chicken breasts

1/4 cup hot sauce

1 tablespoon olive oil

1 teaspoon garlic powder

1/2 teaspoon onion powder

1/2 teaspoon paprika

Salt and pepper to taste

1 head iceberg lettuce

1/2 cup diced celery

1/2 cup crumbled blue cheese

Ranch or blue cheese dressing for serving

Directions

1. Preheat the oven to 375°F (190°C).
2. In a mixing bowl, whisk together the hot sauce, olive oil, garlic powder, onion powder, paprika, salt, and pepper.
3. Add the chicken breasts to the bowl and toss to coat with the mixture.
4. Place the chicken breasts on a baking sheet and bake in the preheated oven for 20-25 minutes or until cooked through.
5. Remove the chicken from the oven and let it cool for a few minutes.
6. Use a fork or your hands to shred the chicken into small pieces.
7. Wash and dry the lettuce leaves and use them as the wraps for the chicken.
8. Top the chicken with the diced celery and crumbled blue cheese.
9. Drizzle with ranch or blue cheese dressing to serve.
10. Enjoy your low-carb Buffalo Chicken Lettuce Wraps!

CHEESY BROCCOLI CASSEROLE

Ingredients:

- 4 cups fresh broccoli florets
- 2 tbsp butter
- 2 cloves garlic, minced
- 1/4 cup diced onion
- 4 oz cream cheese, softened
- 1/4 cup heavy cream
- 1/4 cup chicken broth
- 1 cup shredded cheddar cheese
- Salt and pepper to taste

Procedure:

1. Preheat oven to 375°F (190°C).
2. Steam the broccoli florets for about 5-7 minutes until slightly tender, but still crisp.
3. In a saucepan, melt the butter over medium heat. Add minced garlic and diced onion, cook until the onion is translucent.
4. Add the softened cream cheese, heavy cream, and chicken broth to the saucepan. Stir until the cream cheese has melted and the mixture is smooth.
5. Add shredded cheddar cheese, salt, and pepper to the saucepan. Stir until the cheese has melted.
6. In a baking dish, spread the steamed broccoli florets in a single layer. Pour the cheese sauce over the broccoli.
7. Bake in the preheated oven for 20-25 minutes, or until the top is golden brown and bubbly.
8. Serve hot and enjoy!

BAKED SALMON WITH LEMON BUTTER SAUCE

INGREDIENTS

4 salmon fillets

Salt and black pepper, to taste

1/4 cup unsalted butter, melted

1/4 cup fresh lemon juice

1 tablespoon minced garlic

1 tablespoon chopped fresh parsley

DIRECTIONS

1. Preheat the oven to 375°F (190°C).
2. Season the salmon fillets with salt and black pepper, to taste.
3. In a small mixing bowl, whisk together the melted butter, lemon juice, and minced garlic.
4. Place the salmon fillets in a baking dish and pour the lemon butter sauce over them.
5. Bake for 15-20 minutes or until the salmon is cooked through.
6. Remove from the oven and sprinkle with chopped fresh parsley.
7. Serve hot and enjoy!

Cucumber Avocado Salad

Ingredients

2 cucumbers, sliced
2 ripe avocados, cubed
1/4 red onion, thinly
sliced
1/4 cup fresh cilantro,
chopped
1 lime, juiced
2 tablespoons olive oil
Salt and pepper, to taste

Method

1. In a large bowl, combine the sliced cucumbers, cubed avocados, sliced red onion, and chopped cilantro.
2. In a small bowl, whisk together the lime juice, olive oil, salt, and pepper.
3. Pour the dressing over the salad and toss to combine.
4. Serve chilled.

Eggplant Parmesan

Ingredients

1 large eggplant, sliced into rounds

2 cups of lowcarb marinara sauce

1 cup of almond flour

1/2 cup of grated parmesan cheese

2 eggs, beaten

2 tbsp olive oil

1 tsp garlic powder

1 tsp dried basil

1 tsp dried oregano

Salt and pepper, to taste

1 cup shredded mozzarella cheese

Directions

1. Preheat your oven to 400°F (200°C).

2. In a shallow bowl, mix together the almond flour, parmesan cheese, garlic powder, basil, oregano, salt, and pepper.

3. Dip the eggplant rounds in the beaten eggs, then coat them in the almond flour mixture.

4. In a large skillet, heat the olive oil over medium-high heat. Add the eggplant rounds and cook until golden brown on both sides, about 3-4 minutes per side.

5. Transfer the cooked eggplant rounds to a 9x13 inch baking dish.

6. Spread the marinara sauce over the eggplant rounds, then sprinkle with shredded mozzarella cheese.

7. Bake in the preheated oven for 15-20 minutes, until the cheese is melted and bubbly.

8. Let cool for a few minutes before serving.

CAULIFLOWER PIZZA CRUST

Ingredients:

- 1 medium head cauliflower, cut into small florets
- 1/2 cup shredded mozzarella cheese
- 1/4 cup grated Parmesan cheese
- 1/2 teaspoon dried oregano
- 1/2 teaspoon garlic powder
- 1/4 teaspoon salt
- 2 eggs, lightly beaten

Instructions:

1. Preheat oven to 425°F (220°C).
2. Place cauliflower florets in a food processor and pulse until finely chopped, resembling rice.
3. Microwave the cauliflower rice in a microwave-safe bowl for 5-8 minutes, or until tender. Let it cool.
4. Place the cooled cauliflower rice in a clean kitchen towel and squeeze out as much moisture as possible.
5. In a mixing bowl, combine the cauliflower rice, mozzarella cheese, Parmesan cheese, oregano, garlic powder, salt, and eggs until well blended.
6. Line a baking sheet with parchment paper and spread the cauliflower mixture into a circle or rectangle (depending on the shape of your baking sheet) about 1/4 inch thick.
7. Bake for 10-12 minutes, or until the crust is set and lightly browned.
8. Remove from oven and add your desired pizza toppings.
9. Return the pizza to the oven and bake for an additional 5-7 minutes, or until the cheese is melted and bubbly.
10. Let it cool for a few minutes before slicing and serving.

GRILLED RIBEYE STEAK

INGREDIENTS

2 Ribeye steaks (1 1/2-inch thick)

2 tablespoons olive oil

1 tablespoon garlic powder

1 tablespoon onion powder

1 tablespoon smoked paprika

1 tablespoon sea salt

1 tablespoon black pepper

DIRECTIONS

1. Preheat grill to high heat.
2. In a small bowl, combine olive oil, garlic powder, onion powder, smoked paprika, sea salt, and black pepper. Mix well.
3. Rub the spice mixture all over the ribeye steaks.
4. Place the steaks on the grill and cook for 6-8 minutes per side for medium-rare.
5. Remove from the grill and let rest for 5 minutes.
6. Slice the steak and serve with your favorite low carb side dish.
7. Enjoy your grilled ribeye steak!

Spicy Shrimp Stir Fry

Ingredients

1 lb large shrimp, peeled and deveined
2 tbsp. vegetable oil
2 cloves garlic, minced
1 red bell pepper, sliced
1 green bell pepper, sliced
1 small onion, sliced
1 tbsp. soy sauce
1 tbsp. oyster sauce
1 tbsp. chili garlic sauce
Salt and pepper to taste
Green onions, sliced (for garnish)

Method

1. Heat a large skillet over medium-high heat. Add the vegetable oil and garlic, and stir fry for about 30 seconds until fragrant.

2. Add the shrimp to the skillet and stir fry for about 2-3 minutes until they turn pink and start to curl. Remove the shrimp from the skillet and set aside.

3. Add the sliced bell peppers and onion to the skillet, and stir fry for about 3-4 minutes until they start to soften.

4. Add the soy sauce, oyster sauce, and chili garlic sauce to the skillet, and stir fry for another 1-2 minutes until the vegetables are coated with the sauce.

5. Return the shrimp to the skillet and stir fry for another minute until everything is heated through. Season with salt and pepper to taste.

6. Serve the spicy shrimp stir fry hot, garnished with sliced green onions.

7. Enjoy your delicious and low carb Spicy Shrimp Stir Fry!

Chicken Fajita
Bowl

Ingredients

For the chicken:

1 lb boneless, skinless chicken breast, cut into strips

1 tbsp olive oil

1 tbsp chili powder

1 tsp ground cumin

1 tsp smoked paprika

1/2 tsp garlic powder

1/2 tsp onion powder

Salt and pepper to taste

For the bowl:

1 red bell pepper, sliced

1 green bell pepper, sliced

1 small onion, sliced

1 tbsp olive oil

Salt and pepper to taste

4 cups cauliflower rice

1 avocado, sliced

Fresh cilantro, chopped (optional)

Directions

1. In a bowl, mix together the chili powder, cumin, smoked paprika, garlic powder, onion powder, salt, and pepper. Add the chicken strips and coat well.

2. In a large skillet over medium-high heat, heat the olive oil. Add the chicken strips and cook for about 5-6 minutes per side, until browned and cooked through. Remove from the skillet and set aside.

3. In the same skillet, add the bell peppers, onion, olive oil, salt, and pepper. Cook for about 5-6 minutes, until the vegetables are tender and slightly charred.

4. In another skillet, cook the cauliflower rice until heated through and slightly browned.

5. To assemble the bowls, divide the cauliflower rice among four bowls. Add the cooked chicken and vegetables on top. Top with sliced avocado and chopped cilantro, if desired.

6. Serve hot and enjoy your delicious and low carb Chicken Fajita Bowl!

CAULIFLOWER
MAC AND CHEESE

Ingredients:

- 1 head of cauliflower, chopped into small florets
- 2 tbsp butter
- 2 tbsp almond flour
- 1 cup unsweetened almond milk
- 1 cup grated cheddar cheese
- 1/4 cup grated Parmesan cheese
- 1 tsp Dijon mustard
- Salt and pepper to taste
- Optional: chopped fresh parsley for garnish

Procedure:

1. Preheat the oven to 375°F.
2. In a large pot of boiling salted water, cook the cauliflower florets for 5-7 minutes, or until tender but not mushy. Drain well and set aside.
3. In a saucepan over medium heat, melt the butter. Add the almond flour and whisk to combine. Cook for 1-2 minutes until lightly browned and fragrant.
4. Add the almond milk to the saucepan and whisk until smooth. Cook for 2-3 minutes, or until the mixture begins to thicken.
5. Add the grated cheddar cheese, Parmesan cheese, Dijon mustard, salt, and pepper to the saucepan. Whisk until the cheese has melted and the sauce is smooth.
6. Add the cooked cauliflower to the saucepan and stir until the cauliflower is evenly coated with the cheese sauce.
7. Transfer the mixture to an oven-safe baking dish and bake for 15-20 minutes, or until the top is lightly browned and bubbly.
8. Garnish with chopped fresh parsley, if desired, and serve hot.
9. Enjoy your delicious and low carb Cauliflower Mac and Cheese!

LOW-CARB MEATBALLS WITH MARINARA SAUCE

INGREDIENTS

For the meatballs:
1 lb. ground beef (or a mix of beef and pork)
1/2 cup almond flour
1/4 cup grated Parmesan cheese
2 cloves garlic, minced
1 egg
1 tsp dried oregano
1 tsp dried basil
1/2 tsp salt
1/4 tsp black pepper
For the marinara sauce:
1 tbsp olive oil
1 small onion, chopped
2 cloves garlic, minced
1 can (14 oz.) crushed tomatoes
1 tsp dried basil
1/2 tsp dried oregano
Salt and pepper to taste

DIRECTIONS

1. Preheat the oven to 400°F.
2. In a large bowl, mix together the ground beef, almond flour, Parmesan cheese, garlic, egg, oregano, basil, salt, and pepper. Use your hands to mix until well combined.
3. Form the mixture into 1-1/2 inch meatballs and place them on a baking sheet lined with parchment paper.
4. Bake the meatballs in the preheated oven for 20-25 minutes, or until they are browned and cooked through.
5. While the meatballs are baking, make the marinara sauce. In a saucepan over medium heat, heat the olive oil. Add the chopped onion and garlic and cook for 2-3 minutes, or until the onion is translucent.
6. Add the crushed tomatoes, basil, oregano, salt, and pepper to the saucepan. Stir well to combine and bring to a simmer.
7. Reduce the heat to low and let the sauce simmer for 10-15 minutes, or until it has thickened slightly.
8. Once the meatballs are done, transfer them to a large bowl and pour the marinara sauce over them. Gently stir to coat the meatballs with the sauce.
9. Serve hot and enjoy your delicious low-carb meatballs with marinara sauce!

Asparagus with Parmesan Crust

Ingredients

1 lb asparagus, trimmed
1/4 cup almond flour
1/4 cup grated Parmesan cheese
1/4 tsp garlic powder
Salt and pepper to taste
1 egg, lightly beaten
1 tbsp olive oil

Method

1. Preheat the oven to 400°F.
2. In a shallow bowl, mix together the almond flour, grated Parmesan cheese, garlic powder, salt, and pepper.
3. Dip each asparagus spear into the beaten egg, then roll it in the almond flour mixture until evenly coated.
4. Place the coated asparagus spears on a baking sheet lined with parchment paper.
5. Drizzle the olive oil over the asparagus spears.
6. Bake in the preheated oven for 12-15 minutes, or until the asparagus is tender and the Parmesan crust is golden brown.
7. Serve hot and enjoy!

This Asparagus with Parmesan Crust recipe is not only low-carb, but it's also gluten-free and keto-friendly. It makes for a great side dish to any protein, such as chicken, fish, or steak.

Garlic Herb
Roasted Carrots

Ingredients · Directions

1 lb. carrots, peeled and sliced into
1/4 inch rounds
2 tbsp olive oil
2 cloves garlic, minced
1 tsp dried thyme
1 tsp dried rosemary
Salt and pepper to taste

1. Preheat the oven to 400°F.
2. In a large bowl, toss together the
   sliced carrots, olive oil, minced garlic,
   thyme, rosemary, salt, and pepper.
3. Spread the seasoned carrots out in a
   single layer on a baking sheet lined
   with parchment paper.
4. Roast the carrots in the preheated
   oven for 20-25 minutes, or until they
   are tender and lightly browned.
5. Serve hot and enjoy your delicious
   and low-carb Garlic Herb Roasted
   Carrots!

This side dish is perfect for any meal, from weeknight dinners to holiday gatherings. You can also customize the herbs and spices to your liking, such as adding in some paprika or cumin for a smoky flavor

GREEK CHICKEN SALAD

Ingredients:

- For the chicken:
- 1 lb. boneless, skinless chicken breasts
- 1 tbsp olive oil
- 1 tsp dried oregano
- 1/2 tsp garlic powder
- Salt and pepper to taste
- For the salad:
- 4 cups chopped romaine lettuce
- 1 cup diced cucumber
- 1 cup cherry tomatoes, halved
- 1/2 cup diced red onion
- 1/2 cup crumbled feta cheese
- 1/4 cup pitted Kalamata olives
- For the dressing:
- 1/4 cup olive oil
- 2 tbsp red wine vinegar
- 1 tbsp Dijon mustard
- 1 clove garlic, minced
- 1 tsp dried oregano
- Salt and pepper to taste

Procedure:

1. Preheat the oven to 400°F.
2. In a small bowl, mix together the olive oil, dried oregano, garlic powder, salt, and pepper.
3. Place the chicken breasts on a baking sheet lined with parchment paper and brush the seasoned olive oil mixture over both sides of the chicken.
4. Roast the chicken in the preheated oven for 20-25 minutes, or until it is cooked through and no longer pink inside. Let the chicken cool for a few minutes, then slice it into strips.
5. In a large bowl, combine the chopped romaine lettuce, diced cucumber, cherry tomatoes, diced red onion, crumbled feta cheese, and pitted Kalamata olives.
6. In a small bowl, whisk together the olive oil, red wine vinegar, Dijon mustard, minced garlic, dried oregano, salt, and pepper to make the dressing.
7. Drizzle the dressing over the salad and toss well to combine.
8. Top the salad with the sliced chicken and serve immediately.

BROCCOLI CHEDDAR SOUP

INGREDIENTS

4 cups broccoli florets

4 cups chicken broth

1 cup heavy cream

1 cup shredded cheddar cheese

1/4 cup grated Parmesan cheese

2 tbsp butter

1 small onion, chopped

2 cloves garlic, minced

Salt and pepper to taste

DIRECTIONS

1. In a large pot or Dutch oven, melt the butter over medium heat.

2. Add the chopped onion and minced garlic and sauté for 2-3 minutes, or until the onion is translucent.

3. Add the broccoli florets and chicken broth to the pot and bring to a boil.

4. Reduce the heat to low and let the soup simmer for 10-15 minutes, or until the broccoli is tender.

5. Use an immersion blender or transfer the soup to a blender and blend until smooth.

6. Add the heavy cream, shredded cheddar cheese, and grated Parmesan cheese to the pot and stir until the cheese is melted and the soup is creamy.

7. Season with salt and pepper to taste.

8. Serve hot and enjoy your delicious and low-carb Broccoli Cheddar Soup!

This soup is perfect for a cozy and comforting meal on a chilly day, and it's also great for meal prepping and leftovers. You can also add some crispy bacon or sliced green onions on top for some extra flavor and crunch.

Cheesy Brussels Sprouts Casserole

Ingredients

2 lbs Brussels sprouts, trimmed
and halved

1/2 cup heavy cream

1/2 cup chicken broth

1/2 cup grated Parmesan
cheese

1/2 cup shredded mozzarella
cheese

4 slices of bacon, cooked and
crumbled

2 cloves garlic, minced

2 tbsp butter

Salt and pepper to taste

Method

1. Preheat the oven to 375°F.
2. In a large skillet, melt the butter over medium heat.
3. Add the minced garlic and sauté for 1-2 minutes, or until fragrant.
4. Add the Brussels sprouts to the skillet and cook for 5-7 minutes, or until they are lightly browned and tender.
5. Season the Brussels sprouts with salt and pepper to taste.
6. In a small bowl, whisk together the heavy cream and chicken broth.
7. Pour the cream mixture over the Brussels sprouts and stir to combine.
8. Sprinkle the grated Parmesan cheese and shredded mozzarella cheese over the top of the Brussels sprouts.
9. Bake the casserole in the preheated oven for 20-25 minutes, or until the cheese is melted and bubbly.
10. Sprinkle the crumbled bacon over the top of the casserole and serve hot.

Stuffed Portobello Mushrooms

Ingredients

4 large Portobello mushroom caps

1 lb ground turkey or chicken

1/2 cup chopped onion

1/2 cup chopped bell pepper

2 cloves garlic, minced

1/2 cup chopped tomatoes

1/2 cup grated Parmesan cheese

1 tbsp olive oil

Salt and pepper to taste

Fresh parsley, chopped (for garnish)

Directions

1. Preheat the oven to 375°F.
2. Remove the stems from the Portobello mushrooms and clean them using a damp cloth.
3. In a large skillet, heat the olive oil over medium heat.
4. Add the ground turkey or chicken to the skillet and cook for 5-7 minutes, or until browned.
5. Add the chopped onion, bell pepper, and garlic to the skillet and cook for an additional 3-4 minutes, or until the vegetables are tender.
6. Add the chopped tomatoes to the skillet and stir to combine.
7. Remove the skillet from heat and stir in the grated Parmesan cheese.
8. Season the turkey or chicken mixture with salt and pepper to taste.
9. Spoon the mixture into each Portobello mushroom cap, filling each one evenly.
10. Place the stuffed mushrooms on a baking sheet and bake in the preheated oven for 15-20 minutes, or until the mushrooms are tender and the filling is heated through.
11. Sprinkle fresh parsley over the top of the stuffed mushrooms and serve hot.

LEMON BUTTER COD

Ingredients:

- 4 cod fillets
- 4 tbsp unsalted butter, melted
- 2 tbsp fresh lemon juice
- 1 tsp lemon zest
- 2 cloves garlic, minced
- Salt and pepper to taste
- Fresh parsley, chopped (for garnish)

Procedure:

1. Preheat the oven to 375°F.
2. Season the cod fillets with salt and pepper and place them in a baking dish.
3. In a small bowl, whisk together the melted butter, fresh lemon juice, lemon zest, and minced garlic.
4. Pour the lemon butter mixture over the cod fillets, making sure they are coated evenly.
5. Bake the cod fillets in the preheated oven for 15-20 minutes, or until the fish is cooked through and flakes easily with a fork.
6. Garnish with fresh parsley and serve hot.

SPINACH AND FETA STUFFED CHICKEN

INGREDIENTS

4 boneless, skinless chicken breasts

1 cup fresh spinach, chopped

1/2 cup crumbled feta cheese

2 cloves garlic, minced

2 tbsp olive oil

Salt and pepper to taste

Toothpicks

DIRECTIONS

1. Preheat the oven to 375°F.
2. Using a sharp knife, carefully cut a pocket into each chicken breast.
3. In a small mixing bowl, combine the chopped spinach, crumbled feta cheese, minced garlic, and olive oil.
4. Stuff each chicken breast with the spinach and feta mixture, using toothpicks to secure the opening.
5. Season the chicken breasts with salt and pepper to taste.
6. Heat a large skillet over medium-high heat.
7. Add the stuffed chicken breasts to the skillet and cook for 3-4 minutes on each side, or until golden brown.
8. Transfer the chicken breasts to a baking dish and bake in the preheated oven for 20-25 minutes, or until the chicken is cooked through and no longer pink.
9. Remove the toothpicks before serving.

This Spinach and Feta Stuffed Chicken recipe is a perfect low-carb meal that is both delicious and easy to make. The combination of fresh spinach and tangy feta cheese creates a flavorful and healthy stuffing for the tender and juicy chicken breasts. You can also experiment with different herbs and spices to create your own unique stuffed chicken recipe.

Low-Carb Chicken Enchiladas

Ingredients

4 large zucchinis
2 cups shredded cooked
    chicken
1/2 cup diced onion
2 cloves garlic, minced
1 cup enchilada sauce
1 cup shredded cheddar cheese
1 tbsp olive oil
Salt and pepper to taste
Fresh cilantro (for garnish)

Method

1. Preheat the oven to 375°F.
2. Using a vegetable peeler, peel the zucchinis into thin slices lengthwise.
3. In a large skillet, heat the olive oil over medium heat.
4. Add the diced onion and minced garlic and sauté until softened, about 3-4 minutes.
5. Add the shredded chicken and stir until heated through
6. Add 1/2 cup of the enchilada sauce to the chicken mixture and stir until combined.
7. Spread a spoonful of the remaining enchilada sauce onto the bottom of a baking dish
8. Take a slice of zucchini and place a spoonful of the chicken mixture onto it. Roll it up and place it seam-side down in the baking dish. Repeat with the remaining zucchini slices and chicken mixture.
9. Pour the remaining enchilada sauce over the top of the zucchini rolls, and sprinkle the shredded cheddar cheese over the top.
10. Bake in the preheated oven for 25-30 minutes, or until the cheese is melted and bubbly.
11. Garnish with fresh cilantro before serving.

Cauliflower Alfredo with Bacon and Peas

Ingredients

1 large head cauliflower, chopped

4 slices bacon, chopped

1/2 cup frozen peas

2 cloves garlic, minced

1/4 cup heavy cream

1/4 cup grated Parmesan cheese

Salt and pepper, to taste

1 tablespoon olive oil

Directions

1. Preheat your oven to 400°F (200°C).

2. Place the chopped cauliflower in a large mixing bowl and drizzle with olive oil. Toss to coat.

3. Spread the cauliflower on a baking sheet and roast for 25-30 minutes, or until tender and lightly browned.

4. In a large skillet, cook the chopped bacon until crispy. Remove the bacon from the pan and set aside, leaving the bacon fat in the pan.

5. Add the minced garlic to the bacon fat and sauté for 1-2 minutes, or until fragrant.

6. Add the frozen peas to the skillet and cook until heated through.

7. Add the roasted cauliflower to the skillet and toss to combine.

8. Pour the heavy cream over the cauliflower and stir to combine.

9. Sprinkle the grated Parmesan cheese over the cauliflower and stir to combine.

10. Add the cooked bacon to the skillet and toss to combine.

11. Season with salt and pepper, to taste.

12. Serve the cauliflower Alfredo hot and enjoy!

This recipe makes 4 servings of cauliflower Alfredo with bacon and peas, with approximately 6 grams of net carbs per serving. Enjoy your delicious and low-carb meal.

Roasted Brussels Sprouts
with Garlic Parmesan

Ingredients

1 pound Brussels sprouts,
trimmed and halved
2 tablespoons olive oil
3 cloves garlic, minced
1/4 cup grated Parmesan
cheese
Salt and pepper, to taste

Method

1 Preheat your oven to 400°F (200°C).
2 In a large mixing bowl, toss the Brussels sprouts with
olive oil, minced garlic, salt, and pepper until they
are evenly coated.
3 Spread the Brussels sprouts in a single layer on a
baking sheet and roast for 20-25 minutes, or until
they are tender and golden brown.
4 Remove the Brussels sprouts from the oven and
sprinkle them with grated Parmesan cheese.
5 Return the Brussels sprouts to the oven and continue
roasting for another 3-5 minutes, or until the cheese
is melted and bubbly.
6 Serve the roasted Brussels sprouts hot and enjoy!

This recipe makes 4 servings of roasted Brussels sprouts with garlic Parmesan, with
approximately 6 grams of net carbs per serving. It's a delicious and nutritious low-carb
side dish that pairs well with any main course. Enjoy!

GRILLED SHRIMP SKEWERS

INGREDIENTS

1 pound large shrimp, peeled and deveined

1/4 cup olive oil

2 tablespoons fresh lemon juice

2 cloves garlic, minced

1 teaspoon smoked paprika

1/2 teaspoon cumin

Salt and pepper, to taste

4-6 wooden skewers, soaked in water for 30 minutes

DIRECTIONS

1. In a large mixing bowl, whisk together olive oil, lemon juice, minced garlic, smoked paprika, cumin, salt, and pepper until well combined.

2. Add the shrimp to the marinade and toss to coat evenly. Cover the bowl and refrigerate for at least 30 minutes, or up to 2 hours.

3. Preheat your grill to medium-high heat.

4. Thread the marinated shrimp onto the soaked wooden skewers, leaving a small gap between each shrimp.

5. Place the shrimp skewers on the grill and cook for 2-3 minutes per side, or until they are pink and opaque.

6. Remove the shrimp skewers from the grill and serve hot.

This recipe makes 4 servings of grilled shrimp skewers, with approximately 1 gram of net carbs per serving. It's a healthy and delicious low-carb meal that's perfect for a summer barbecue or a quick weeknight dinner. Enjoy!

BROILED LOBSTER TAILS WITH GARLIC BUTTER

Ingredients:

- 2 lobster tails
- 4 tablespoons unsalted butter, melted
- 2 cloves garlic, minced
- Salt and pepper, to taste
- 1 tablespoon chopped fresh parsley

Procedure:

1. Preheat your broiler to high heat.
2. Using kitchen shears, cut the top of the lobster shell down the middle to expose the meat.
3. Using a sharp knife, carefully cut through the meat to create two halves of the lobster tail.
4. In a small mixing bowl, whisk together melted butter, minced garlic, salt, and pepper until well combined.
5. Brush the garlic butter mixture generously over the lobster tails.
6. Place the lobster tails on a baking sheet and broil for 8-10 minutes, or until the meat is opaque and cooked through.
7. Remove the lobster tails from the oven and sprinkle with chopped fresh parsley.
8. Serve the broiled lobster tails hot with any remaining garlic butter on the side.

Creamy Garlic Butter Tuscan Shrimp

Ingredients

1 pound large shrimp, peeled and deveined

4 tablespoons unsalted butter

4 cloves garlic, minced

1/2 cup heavy cream

1/2 cup chicken broth

1/2 cup grated Parmesan cheese

1 teaspoon dried oregano

1 teaspoon dried basil

Salt and pepper, to taste

1 tablespoon chopped fresh parsley

Directions

1. In a large skillet, melt the butter over medium heat.

2. Add the minced garlic to the skillet and sauté for 1-2 minutes, or until fragrant.

3. Add the shrimp to the skillet and cook for 2-3 minutes per side, or until they are pink and opaque. Remove the shrimp from the skillet and set aside.

4. In the same skillet, add heavy cream, chicken broth, grated Parmesan cheese, dried oregano, and dried basil. Stir to combine.

5. Simmer the sauce for 5-7 minutes, or until it thickens and reduces by about half.

6. Add the cooked shrimp back to the skillet and toss to coat in the sauce.

7. Season with salt and pepper, to taste.

8. Sprinkle chopped fresh parsley over the top of the shrimp and serve hot.

Roasted Cauliflower
with Tahini Sauce

Ingredients

1 head cauliflower, cut into
bite-sized florets
2 tablespoons olive oil
Salt and pepper, to taste
1/4 cup tahini
2 tablespoons fresh lemon
juice
2 cloves garlic, minced
1/4 cup water
1/4 teaspoon ground cumin
1/4 teaspoon paprika
Salt, to taste
Chopped fresh parsley, for
garnish

Method

1 Preheat your oven to 400°F (200°C).

2 In a large mixing bowl, toss the cauliflower florets
with olive oil, salt, and pepper until they are evenly
coated.

3 Spread the cauliflower in a single layer on a baking
sheet and roast for 20-25 minutes, or until they are
tender and golden brown.

4 In a separate mixing bowl, whisk together tahini,
fresh lemon juice, minced garlic, water, ground
cumin, paprika, and salt until well combined.

5 When the cauliflower is finished roasting, transfer it
to a serving dish and drizzle the tahini sauce over the
top.

6 Garnish with chopped fresh parsley and serve hot.

This recipe makes 4 servings of roasted cauliflower with tahini sauce, with approximately 5
grams of net carbs per serving. It's a delicious and healthy low-carb side dish that's full of
flavor and nutrients. Enjoy!

LEMON GARLIC BUTTER SHRIMP AND BROCCOLI

INGREDIENTS

1 pound large shrimp, peeled and deveined

4 tablespoons unsalted butter

4 cloves garlic, minced

1/4 cup fresh lemon juice

Salt and pepper, to taste

2 cups broccoli florets

DIRECTIONS

1. In a large skillet, melt the butter over medium heat.
2. Add the minced garlic to the skillet and sauté for 1-2 minutes, or until fragrant.
3. Add the shrimp to the skillet and cook for 2-3 minutes per side, or until they are pink and opaque. Remove the shrimp from the skillet and set aside.
4. In the same skillet, add the broccoli florets and cook for 3-4 minutes, or until they are tender-crisp.
5. Add the lemon juice to the skillet and stir to combine.
6. Season with salt and pepper, to taste.
7. Add the cooked shrimp back to the skillet and toss to coat in the lemon garlic butter sauce.
8. Serve the shrimp and broccoli hot.

This recipe makes 4 servings of lemon garlic butter shrimp and broccoli, with approximately 6 grams of net carbs per serving. It's a simple and flavorful low-carb meal that's perfect for a quick and easy dinner.

CAPRESE STUFFED AVOCADO

Ingredients:

- 2 ripe avocados, halved and pitted
- 1 cup cherry tomatoes, halved
- 1/2 cup fresh mozzarella balls, halved
- 2 tablespoons chopped fresh basil
- 2 tablespoons balsamic vinegar
- 2 tablespoons olive oil
- Salt and pepper, to taste

Procedure:

1. In a mixing bowl, combine cherry tomatoes, fresh mozzarella balls, chopped fresh basil, balsamic vinegar, olive oil, salt, and pepper. Toss to combine.
2. Scoop the caprese salad mixture into the halved and pitted avocado halves.
3. Serve the caprese stuffed avocado immediately.

Low-Carb Pizza with Cauliflower Crust

Ingredients

1 head cauliflower, cut into florets

1 egg

1/4 cup grated parmesan cheese

1/4 cup shredded mozzarella cheese

1/4 teaspoon garlic powder

1/4 teaspoon dried oregano

Salt and pepper, to taste

1/2 cup low-carb tomato sauce

1 cup shredded mozzarella cheese

Toppings of your choice (such as pepperoni, mushrooms, bell peppers, etc.)

Directions

1. Preheat your oven to 400°F (200°C)

2. Place the cauliflower florets in a food processor and pulse until they are finely ground.

3. Microwave the cauliflower in a microwave-safe bowl for 5-6 minutes, or until it's cooked and tender.

4. Place the cooked cauliflower in a clean kitchen towel and squeeze out as much moisture as possible.

5. In a mixing bowl, combine the cauliflower, egg, grated parmesan cheese, shredded mozzarella cheese, garlic powder, dried oregano, salt, and pepper. Mix until well combined.

6. Transfer the cauliflower mixture to a baking sheet lined with parchment paper.

7. Use your hands to press the cauliflower mixture into a thin crust shape.

8. Bake the cauliflower crust for 15-20 minutes, or until it's golden brown and crispy.

9. Remove the cauliflower crust from the oven and spread the low-carb tomato sauce over the top.

10. Sprinkle shredded mozzarella cheese and your desired toppings over the tomato sauce.

11. Return the pizza to the oven and bake for an additional 10-15 minutes, or until the cheese is melted and bubbly.

12. Slice the pizza into wedges and serve hot.

13.

Steak Fajita Bowl

Ingredients

1 pound flank steak, sliced
2 bell peppers, sliced
1 onion, sliced
2 tablespoons olive oil
2 teaspoons chili powder
1 teaspoon ground cumin
1 teaspoon garlic powder
Salt and pepper, to taste
4 cups cooked cauliflower rice
Optional toppings: diced avocado, salsa, shredded cheese, sour cream

Method

1. In a mixing bowl, combine the sliced flank steak, sliced bell peppers, sliced onion, olive oil, chili powder, ground cumin, garlic powder, salt, and pepper. Toss to combine.
2. Heat a large skillet over high heat.
3. Add the steak and vegetables to the skillet and cook for 6-8 minutes, or until the steak is cooked to your desired level of doneness and the vegetables are tender-crisp.
4. Divide the cooked cauliflower rice into four bowls.
5. Top each bowl with the steak and vegetables mixture.
6. Garnish with optional toppings, if desired.
7. Serve the steak fajita bowls hot.

BACON WRAPPED ASPARAGUS

INGREDIENTS

1 pound asparagus, trimmed

8-10 slices bacon

Salt and pepper, to taste

DIRECTIONS

1. Preheat your oven to 400°F (200°C).
2. Line a baking sheet with parchment paper.
3. Wrap each asparagus spear with a slice of bacon, starting at the bottom and wrapping around the spear to the top.
4. Place the bacon wrapped asparagus spears on the prepared baking sheet.
5. Season with salt and pepper, to taste.
6. Bake the bacon wrapped asparagus for 15-20 minutes, or until the bacon is crispy and the asparagus is tender.
7. Remove the bacon wrapped asparagus from the oven and serve hot.

This recipe makes 4 servings of bacon wrapped asparagus, with approximately 2 grams of net carbs per serving. It's a simple and delicious low-carb side dish that's perfect for any meal.

GARLIC HERB
BUTTER CHICKEN

Ingredients:

- 2 cups of awesome
- 1/2 tsp of fun
- 3 tbsp color
- 1 cup of kindness
- salt and pepper to taste

Procedure:

1. MPreheat your oven to 460°F (200°C).
2. Line a baking dish with parchment paper.
3. In a mixing bowl, combine the melted butter, minced garlic, chopped fresh thyme, chopped fresh rosemary, salt, and pepper. Mix until well combined.
4. Place the chicken breasts in the prepared baking dish.
5. Brush the garlic herb butter mixture over the top of each chicken breast.
6. Bake the chicken breasts for 20-25 minutes, or until they are cooked through and the juices run clear.
7. Remove the chicken breasts from the oven and let them rest for 5 minutes before slicing.
8. Serve the garlic herb butter chicken hot.

Creamy Tomato Soup

Ingredients

2 tablespoons olive oil

1 onion, chopped

3 cloves garlic, minced

1 can (28 ounces) crushed tomatoes

2 cups chicken broth

1 teaspoon dried basil

1 teaspoon dried oregano

Salt and pepper, to taste

1/4 cup heavy cream

Directions

1. Heat the olive oil in a large pot over medium heat.

2. Add the onion and garlic and cook for 5 minutes, or until the onion is soft and translucent.

3. Add the crushed tomatoes, chicken broth, dried basil, dried oregano, salt, and pepper. Stir to combine.

4. Bring the soup to a simmer and cook for 20-25 minutes, or until the flavors have melded together.

5. Remove the soup from the heat and use an immersion blender to blend it until smooth.

6. Add the heavy cream and stir to combine.

7. Serve the creamy tomato soup hot.

Baked Salmon with Asparagus and Lemon

Ingredients

4 salmon fillets
1 pound asparagus, trimmed
2 tablespoons olive oil
2 cloves garlic, minced
1 lemon, sliced
Salt and pepper, to taste

Method

1. Preheat your oven to 400°F (200°C).
2. Line a baking sheet with parchment paper.
3. Place the salmon fillets on one side of the prepared baking sheet.
4. Place the asparagus on the other side of the prepared baking sheet.
5. Drizzle the olive oil over the salmon and asparagus.
6. Sprinkle the minced garlic over the salmon and asparagus.
7. Arrange the lemon slices over the salmon and asparagus.
8. Season everything with salt and pepper, to taste.
9. Bake the salmon and asparagus for 12-15 minutes, or until the salmon is cooked through and the asparagus is tender.
10. Remove the baked salmon and asparagus from the oven and serve hot.

This recipe makes 4 servings of baked salmon with asparagus and lemon, with approximately 5 grams of net carbs per serving. It's a healthy and delicious low-carb meal that's perfect for a quick and easy dinner.

GREEK STUFFED PEPPERS

INGREDIENTS

4 bell peppers, halved
and seeded

1 pound ground beef

1/2 cup chopped onion

2 cloves garlic, minced

1/2 teaspoon dried
oregano

1/2 teaspoon dried basil

Salt and pepper, to
taste

1/2 cup crumbled feta
cheese

1/4 cup chopped fresh
parsley

DIRECTIONS

1. Preheat your oven to 350°F (175°C).
2. Arrange the bell pepper halves in a baking dish.
3. In a skillet over medium heat, cook the ground beef,
   chopped onion, minced garlic, dried oregano, dried
   basil, salt, and pepper until the beef is browned and
   cooked through.
4. Stir in the crumbled feta cheese and chopped fresh
   parsley.
5. Spoon the beef mixture into the bell pepper halves.
6. Cover the baking dish with foil and bake for 25-30
   minutes, or until the peppers are tender and the
   beef mixture is heated through.
7. Remove the Greek stuffed peppers from the oven
   and serve hot.

This recipe makes 4 servings of Greek stuffed peppers, with

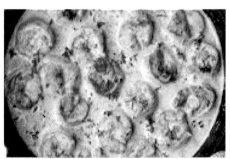

CREAMY GARLIC BUTTER SHRIMP SCAMPI

Ingredients:

- 1 pound large shrimp, peeled and deveined
- 2 tablespoons olive oil
- 3 cloves garlic, minced
- 1/2 cup heavy cream
- 1/4 cup grated Parmesan cheese
- 2 tablespoons butter
- Salt and pepper, to taste
- Chopped fresh parsley, for garnish

Procedure:

1. Heat the olive oil in a large skillet over medium-high heat.
2. Add the minced garlic and cook for 1 minute, or until fragrant.
3. Add the shrimp to the skillet and cook for 2-3 minutes per side, or until pink and cooked through.
4. Remove the cooked shrimp from the skillet and set aside.
5. In the same skillet, add the heavy cream and grated Parmesan cheese. Stir to combine.
6. Add the butter to the skillet and stir until melted.
7. Season the creamy garlic butter sauce with salt and pepper, to taste.
8. Add the cooked shrimp back to the skillet and toss to coat with the sauce.
9. Garnish with chopped fresh parsley and serve hot.

Low-Carb Beef
Stroganoff

Ingredients

1 pound beef sirloin, cut into thin strips

1 onion, chopped

2 cloves garlic, minced

1 cup beef broth

1/2 cup sour cream

2 tablespoons butter

Salt and pepper, to taste

Chopped fresh parsley, for garnish

Directions

1. Heat the butter in a large skillet over medium-high heat.

2. Add the chopped onion and minced garlic and cook for 5 minutes, or until the onion is soft and translucent.

3. Add the beef strips to the skillet and cook for 3-4 minutes per side, or until browned.

4. Remove the cooked beef from the skillet and set aside.

5. In the same skillet, add the beef broth and simmer for 10-15 minutes, or until the liquid has reduced by half.

6. Stir in the sour cream until well combined.

7. Add the cooked beef back to the skillet and toss to coat with the sauce.

8. Season the low-carb beef stroganoff with salt and pepper, to taste.

9. Garnish with chopped fresh parsley and serve hot.

Lemon Garlic Butter Shrimp and Zucchini Noodles

Ingredients

1 pound shrimp, peeled and
deveined

Salt and pepper, to taste

2 tablespoons butter

4 cloves garlic, minced

1/4 cup chicken broth

2 tablespoons lemon juice

2 zucchini, spiralized into
noodles

2 tablespoons chopped fresh
parsley

Method

1. Season the shrimp with salt and pepper, to taste.

2. Heat the butter in a large skillet over medium heat.

3. Add the shrimp to the skillet and cook for 2-3
minutes per side, or until pink and cooked through.
Remove the shrimp from the skillet and set aside.

4. Add the minced garlic to the skillet and cook for 1-2
minutes, or until fragrant.

5. Pour the chicken broth into the skillet and stir to
combine with the garlic.

6. Add the lemon juice and zucchini noodles to the
skillet. Cook for 2-3 minutes, or until the zucchini
noodles are tender.

7. Return the cooked shrimp to the skillet and toss
with the zucchini noodles.

8. Serve the lemon garlic butter shrimp and zucchini
noodles hot, garnished with chopped fresh parsley.

STUFFED BELL PEPPERS WITH GROUND BEEF AND CHEESE

INGREDIENTS

4 bell peppers

1 pound ground beef

1 onion, chopped

2 cloves garlic, minced

1 cup cauliflower rice

1 cup diced tomatoes

1 cup shredded cheddar cheese

1 teaspoon paprika

Salt and pepper, to taste

Olive oil, for cooking

DIRECTIONS

1. Preheat the oven to 375°F.
2. Cut off the tops of the bell peppers and remove the seeds and membranes. Place the peppers in a baking dish and set aside.
3. Heat some olive oil in a large skillet over medium heat.
4. Add the chopped onion and minced garlic to the skillet and cook for 2-3 minutes, or until softened.
5. Add the ground beef to the skillet and cook for 5-7 minutes, or until browned and cooked through.
6. Add the cauliflower rice and diced tomatoes to the skillet. Cook for 2-3 minutes, or until the cauliflower rice is tender.
7. Season the beef mixture with paprika, salt, and pepper, to taste.
8. Stuff the bell peppers with the beef mixture, dividing it evenly between the four peppers.
9. Top each stuffed pepper with shredded cheddar cheese.
10. Bake the stuffed peppers in the preheated oven for 25-30 minutes, or until the cheese is melted and bubbly and the peppers are tender.
11. Remove the stuffed peppers from the oven and let them cool for a few minutes before serving

This recipe makes 4 servings of stuffed bell peppers with ground beef and cheese, with approximately 9 grams of net carbs per serving. It's a hearty and satisfying low-carb meal that's perfect for a weeknight dinner.

ROASTED RADISHES WITH GARLIC BUTTER

Ingredients:

- 1 pound radishes, trimmed and halved
- 2 tablespoons butter
- 2 cloves garlic, minced
- Salt and pepper, to taste

Procedure:

1. Preheat the oven to 400°F.
2. Place the halved radishes on a baking sheet and season with salt and pepper, to taste.
3. Melt the butter in a small saucepan over low heat.
4. Add the minced garlic to the butter and cook for 1-2 minutes, or until fragrant.
5. Pour the garlic butter over the radishes on the baking sheet, tossing to coat.
6. Roast the radishes in the preheated oven for 20-25 minutes, or until tender and golden brown.
7. Serve the roasted radishes with garlic butter hot, garnished with chopped fresh parsley or chives, if desired.

Broiled Cod with

Lemon Butter Sauce

Ingredients

4 cod fillets

Salt and pepper, to taste

1/4 cup butter, melted

2 tablespoons fresh lemon
juice

2 cloves garlic, minced

1 tablespoon chopped fresh
parsley

Method

1. Preheat the broiler.

2. Season the cod fillets with salt and pepper, to taste

3. In a small bowl, whisk together the melted butter, lemon
juice, and minced garlic.

4. Place the seasoned cod fillets on a broiler pan or baking
sheet.

5. Spoon the lemon butter sauce over the cod fillets,
dividing it evenly between them.

6. Broil the cod fillets in the preheated broiler for 8-10
minutes, or until cooked through and flaky.

7. Remove the cod fillets from the broiler and transfer them
to serving plates

8. Drizzle any remaining lemon butter sauce over the cod
fillets

9. Sprinkle chopped fresh parsley over the top of the cod
fillets.

10. Serve the broiled cod with lemon butter sauce hot,
garnished with lemon wedges, if desired.

Stuffed Chicken Breast
with Cream Cheese
and Spinach

Ingredients

4 boneless, skinless chicken
breasts

Salt and pepper, to taste

4 oz cream cheese, softened

1/2 cup frozen chopped spinach,
thawed and drained

2 cloves garlic, minced

1/4 cup grated Parmesan cheese

1/4 teaspoon red pepper flakes

1/4 teaspoon onion powder

1/4 teaspoon dried basil

Toothpicks

Directions

1. Preheat the oven to 375°F.

2. Place the chicken breasts on a cutting board and, using a sharp knife, cut a pocket into the thickest part of each breast.

3. Season the chicken breasts with salt and pepper, to taste.

4. In a medium bowl, combine the softened cream cheese, chopped spinach, minced garlic, grated Parmesan cheese, red pepper flakes, onion powder, and dried basil. Mix well.

5. Spoon the cream cheese and spinach mixture into the pockets of the chicken breasts, dividing it evenly between them.

6. Secure the openings of the chicken breasts with toothpicks.

7. Place the stuffed chicken breasts in a baking dish.

8. Bake the stuffed chicken breasts in the preheated oven for 25-30 minutes, or until cooked through and no longer pink in the center.

9. Remove the toothpicks from the chicken breasts before serving.

10. Serve the stuffed chicken breasts with cream cheese and spinach hot, garnished with chopped fresh parsley, if desired.

GRILLED CHICKEN
CAESAR SALAD

Ingredients:

- 2 boneless, skinless chicken breasts
- Salt and pepper, to taste
- 1 head of Romaine lettuce, washed and chopped
- 1/2 cup grated Parmesan cheese
- 1/2 cup Caesar dressing (look for a low-carb version or make your own)
- 1/4 cup crumbled bacon (optional)
- 1/4 cup sliced black olives (optional)

Procedure:

1. Preheat the grill to medium-high heat.
2. Season the chicken breasts with salt and pepper, to taste.
3. Grill the chicken breasts for 5-6 minutes on each side, or until cooked through.
4. Remove the chicken breasts from the grill and let them rest for 5 minutes.
5. Slice the chicken breasts into thin strips.
6. In a large salad bowl, combine the chopped Romaine lettuce, grated Parmesan cheese, crumbled bacon, and sliced black olives (if using).
7. Add the sliced chicken breast to the salad bowl.
8. Drizzle the Caesar dressing over the salad, and toss to combine.
9. Serve the grilled chicken Caesar salad immediately, garnished with additional Parmesan cheese and black pepper, if desired

CAULIFLOWER RICE AND SAUSAGE SKILLET

INGREDIENTS

1 lb ground sausage
1 head of cauliflower, riced
1 small onion, diced
1 red bell pepper, diced
2 cloves garlic, minced
2 tablespoons olive oil
Salt and pepper, to taste
Optional: chopped fresh parsley or green onions for garnish

DIRECTIONS

1. In a large skillet, heat the olive oil over medium-high heat.
2. Add the ground sausage to the skillet and cook, stirring occasionally, until browned and cooked through, about 8-10 minutes.
3. Remove the sausage from the skillet with a slotted spoon and set it aside on a plate.
4. Add the diced onion, red bell pepper, and minced garlic to the same skillet. Sauté the vegetables for 3-4 minutes, or until they are tender.
5. Add the riced cauliflower to the skillet with the vegetables. Stir to combine.
6. Cook the cauliflower rice for 5-7 minutes, stirring occasionally, or until it is tender and lightly browned.
7. Add the cooked sausage back to the skillet with the cauliflower rice. Stir to combine.
8. Season the skillet with salt and pepper, to taste.
9. Garnish with chopped fresh parsley or green onions, if desired.

Creamy Garlic
Mushroom Chicken

Ingredients

4 boneless, skinless chicken
breasts

Salt and pepper, to taste

2 tablespoons olive oil

8 ounces sliced mushrooms

2 cloves garlic, minced

1 cup chicken broth

1/2 cup heavy cream

1/4 cup grated Parmesan
cheese

1 tablespoon chopped fresh
parsley

Method

1. Season the chicken breasts with salt and pepper, to taste.

2. In a large skillet, heat the olive oil over medium-high
heat.

3. Add the chicken breasts to the skillet and cook for 6-7
minutes on each side, or until cooked through and
golden brown. Remove the chicken from the skillet and
set it aside on a plate.

4. Add the sliced mushrooms and minced garlic to the
same skillet. Sauté the mushrooms for 2-3 minutes, or
until they are tender and lightly browned.

5. Add the chicken broth to the skillet and bring it to a
simmer.

6. Stir in the heavy cream and grated Parmesan cheese.
Cook the sauce for 2-3 minutes, or until it has thickened
slightly.

7. Return the chicken to the skillet with the sauce. Spoon
the sauce over the chicken to coat it evenly.

8. Garnish the skillet with chopped fresh parsley.

Broccoli and Cheese
Stuffed Chicken Breast

Ingredients

4 boneless, skinless chicken breasts

Salt and pepper, to taste

1/2 cup steamed broccoli, chopped

1/2 cup shredded cheddar cheese

1/4 cup cream cheese

2 tablespoons butter

1/4 teaspoon garlic powder

1/4 teaspoon onion powder

1/4 teaspoon paprika

Directions

1. Preheat the oven to 375°F.

2. Season the chicken breasts with salt and pepper, to taste.

3. In a medium bowl, mix together the chopped steamed broccoli, shredded cheddar cheese, cream cheese, garlic powder, and onion powder until well combined.

4. Cut a slit in the thickest part of each chicken breast, being careful not to cut all the way through. Stuff each chicken breast with the broccoli and cheese mixture, then use toothpicks to secure the chicken and hold the filling in place.

5. Melt the butter in a large oven-safe skillet over medium-high heat. Add the stuffed chicken breasts to the skillet and sprinkle them with paprika.

6. Cook the chicken for 3-4 minutes on each side, or until golden brown.

7. Transfer the skillet to the preheated oven and bake for 20-25 minutes, or until the chicken is cooked through and the cheese is melted and bubbly.

8. Remove the toothpicks from the chicken breasts and serve hot.

LOW-CARB CHICKEN ALFREDO WITH BROCCOLI

Ingredients:

- 1 pound boneless, skinless chicken breasts, cut into bite-sized pieces
- 1 head of broccoli, cut into florets
- 2 tablespoons olive oil
- Salt and pepper, to taste
- 1/4 cup unsalted butter
- 1 cup heavy cream
- 1/3 cup grated Parmesan cheese
- 2 cloves garlic, minced
- 1 teaspoon Italian seasoning
- 1/2 teaspoon garlic powder
- 1/4 teaspoon black pepper

Procedure:

1. In a large skillet, heat the olive oil over medium-high heat. Add the chicken pieces and season with salt and pepper, to taste. Cook until golden brown and cooked through, about 6-8 minutes. Remove the chicken from the skillet and set it aside.
2. Add the broccoli florets to the same skillet and cook until tender-crisp, about 5-7 minutes. Remove the broccoli from the skillet and set it aside.
3. In the same skillet, melt the butter over medium heat. Add the minced garlic and cook for 1-2 minutes, or until fragrant.
4. Add the heavy cream, Parmesan cheese, Italian seasoning, garlic powder, and black pepper to the skillet. Stir until the sauce is smooth and creamy.
5. Add the cooked chicken and broccoli back to the skillet and stir until everything is coated in the Alfredo sauce.
6. Cook the mixture for 2-3 minutes, or until heated through.
7. Serve hot, garnished with additional Parmesan cheese and chopped fresh parsley, if desired.

SPINACH STUFFED SALMON

INGREDIENTS

4 salmon fillets (6 oz.
each)

2 tablespoons olive oil

2 garlic cloves, minced

2 cups fresh spinach,
chopped

1/4 cup cream cheese,
softened

1/4 cup grated
Parmesan cheese

Salt and pepper, to
taste

Lemon wedges, for
serving

DIRECTIONS

1. Preheat the oven to 375°F.

2. In a large skillet, heat the olive oil over medium heat.
   Add the minced garlic and sauté for 1-2 minutes, or
   until fragrant.

3. Add the chopped spinach to the skillet and cook
   until wilted, about 2-3 minutes. Remove the skillet
   from the heat and let it cool for a few minutes.

4. In a mixing bowl, combine the cream cheese, grated
   Parmesan cheese, and cooked spinach. Stir until the
   mixture is well combined.

5. Using a sharp knife, cut a pocket into the side of
   each salmon fillet. Stuff each fillet with the spinach
   and cheese mixture.

6. Place the stuffed salmon fillets on a baking sheet
   lined with parchment paper. Season each fillet with
   salt and pepper.

7. Bake the salmon fillets for 12-15 minutes, or until the
   fish is cooked through and flaky.

8. Serve the stuffed salmon fillets hot, garnished with
   lemon wedges.

Greek Meatballs with Tzatziki Sauce

Ingredients

For the meatballs:
1 lb. ground beef or lamb
1/4 cup almond flour
1/4 cup chopped fresh parsley
1/4 cup chopped fresh mint
1/4 cup crumbled feta cheese
1 egg
2 cloves garlic, minced
1 tsp dried oregano
Salt and pepper, to taste
Olive oil, for frying
For the tzatziki sauce:
1 cup plain Greek yogurt
1/2 cucumber, peeled and grated
2 cloves garlic, minced
1 tbsp chopped fresh dill
1 tbsp lemon juice
Salt and pepper, to taste

Method

1. In a large mixing bowl, combine the ground meat, almond flour, parsley, mint, feta cheese, egg, garlic, oregano, salt, and pepper. Mix well to combine.

2. Using your hands, form the mixture into small meatballs, about 1 inch in diameter.

3. In a large skillet, heat the olive oil over medium heat. Add the meatballs to the skillet and fry them until they are browned on all sides and cooked through, about 8-10 minutes.

4. While the meatballs are cooking, prepare the tzatziki sauce. In a mixing bowl, combine the Greek yogurt, grated cucumber, garlic, dill, lemon juice, salt, and pepper. Mix well to combine.

5. Serve the meatballs hot, garnished with fresh parsley and accompanied by the tzatziki sauce.

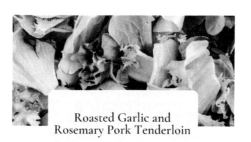

Roasted Garlic and Rosemary Pork Tenderloin

Ingredients

1 lb pork tenderloin

2 cloves garlic, minced

1 tbsp chopped fresh rosemary

1 tsp dried thyme

1 tsp paprika

Salt and pepper, to taste

2 tbsp olive oil

Directions

1. Preheat the oven to 375°F.

2. In a small mixing bowl, combine the minced garlic, chopped rosemary, dried thyme, paprika, salt, and pepper.

3. Rub the pork tenderloin with the olive oil, then coat it with the garlic and herb mixture. Make sure to evenly coat the entire pork tenderloin.

4. Place the pork tenderloin on a baking sheet lined with parchment paper or a baking rack. Roast in the oven for 25-30 minutes, or until the internal temperature of the pork reaches 145°F.

5. Once the pork tenderloin is cooked, remove it from the oven and allow it to rest for 5-10 minutes before slicing it. This will help the juices to distribute evenly throughout the meat.

6. Serve the roasted garlic and rosemary pork tenderloin hot, garnished with fresh rosemary or parsley if desired

This recipe makes approximately 4 servings of roasted garlic and rosemary pork tenderloin, with approximately 3 grams of net carbs per serving. It's a delicious and savory low-carb meal that's perfect for anyone who loves the taste of pork tenderloin.

GARLIC BUTTER SHRIMP AND CAULIFLOWER RICE

Ingredients:

- 1 lb large shrimp, peeled and deveined
- 3 cloves garlic, minced
- 1/4 cup unsalted butter
- 2 tbsp fresh parsley, chopped
- Salt and pepper, to taste
- 1 large head cauliflower, riced
- 2 tbsp olive oil

Procedure:

1. In a large skillet, melt the butter over medium heat. Add the minced garlic and cook for 1-2 minutes until fragrant.
2. Add the shrimp to the skillet and cook for 2-3 minutes on each side, or until they are pink and cooked through.
3. Season the shrimp with salt, pepper, and chopped parsley, then remove them from the skillet and set them aside.
4. In the same skillet, heat the olive oil over medium heat. Add the riced cauliflower to the skillet and cook for 5-7 minutes, or until it's tender and lightly browned.
5. Season the cauliflower rice with salt and pepper to taste.
6. Serve the garlic butter shrimp on top of the cauliflower rice, garnished with additional chopped parsley if desired.

LOW-CARB PHILLY CHEESESTEAK STUFFED PEPPERS

INGREDIENTS

4 large bell peppers, halved and seeded

1 lb thinly sliced beef steak or roast beef

1 green bell pepper, sliced

1 onion, sliced

8 slices provolone cheese

2 tbsp olive oil

Salt and pepper, to taste

DIRECTIONS

1. Preheat your oven to 375°F.
2. Place the halved and seeded bell peppers in a baking dish, then set them aside.
3. In a large skillet, heat the olive oil over medium-high heat. Add the sliced beef and cook until it's browned and cooked through.
4. Add the sliced green bell pepper and onion to the skillet, and cook until they're tender and lightly browned.
5. Season the beef and vegetables with salt and pepper to taste.
6. Spoon the beef and vegetable mixture into the halved bell peppers, filling each pepper half with the mixture.
7. Place a slice of provolone cheese on top of each pepper half.
8. Bake the stuffed peppers in the oven for 15-20 minutes, or until the cheese is melted and bubbly.
9. Remove the stuffed peppers from the oven and let them cool for a few minutes before serving.

Baked Chicken with Asparagus and Roasted Tomatoes

Ingredients

4 boneless, skinless chicken
breasts
1 lb asparagus, trimmed
1 pint cherry tomatoes
2 tbsp olive oil
2 cloves garlic, minced
1 tbsp dried Italian seasoning
Salt and pepper, to taste

Method

1. Preheat your oven to 400°F.
2. Place the chicken breasts in a baking dish, then set them aside.
3. Arrange the trimmed asparagus and cherry tomatoes around the chicken in the baking dish.
4. In a small bowl, whisk together the olive oil, minced garlic, dried Italian seasoning, salt, and pepper.
5. Pour the olive oil mixture over the chicken, asparagus, and cherry tomatoes, making sure to coat everything evenly.
6. Bake the chicken and vegetables in the oven for 25-30 minutes, or until the chicken is cooked through and the vegetables are tender.
7. Remove the baking dish from the oven and let it cool for a few minutes before serving.

This recipe makes approximately 4 servings of Baked Chicken with Asparagus and Roasted Tomatoes, with approximately 5 grams of net carbs per serving. It's a flavorful and healthy low-carb meal that's easy to make and perfect for busy weeknights. Enjoy!

Creamy Garlic Parmesan Shrimp

Ingredients

1 lb shrimp, peeled and deveined
1 tbsp butter
2 cloves garlic, minced
1/2 cup heavy cream
1/2 cup grated Parmesan cheese
Salt and pepper, to taste
Fresh parsley, chopped, for garnish

Directions

1. Melt the butter in a large skillet over medium heat.
2. Add the minced garlic to the skillet and sauté for 1-2 minutes, or until fragrant.
3. Add the shrimp to the skillet and cook until pink and opaque, about 3-4 minutes.
4. Remove the shrimp from the skillet and set aside.
5. In the same skillet, add the heavy cream and grated Parmesan cheese.
6. Stir until the cheese is melted and the sauce is smooth and creamy.
7. Add the cooked shrimp back to the skillet and stir until coated with the sauce.
8. Season with salt and pepper, to taste.
9. Garnish with chopped fresh parsley and serve hot.

CAULIFLOWER AND
BROCCOLI GRATIN

Ingredients:

- 1 head cauliflower, chopped into florets
- 1 head broccoli, chopped into florets
- 1/2 cup heavy cream
- 1/2 cup grated Parmesan cheese
- 2 cloves garlic, minced
- 1 tsp dried thyme
- 1 tsp dried rosemary
- Salt and pepper, to taste
- 1/4 cup almond flour
- 2 tbsp butter, melted

Procedure:

1. Preheat the oven to 375°F (190°C). Grease a 9x13 inch baking dish.
2. Steam the cauliflower and broccoli florets for 5-7 minutes, or until slightly tender.
3. In a separate bowl, whisk together the heavy cream, grated Parmesan cheese, minced garlic, dried thyme, dried rosemary, salt, and pepper.
4. Arrange the steamed cauliflower and broccoli in the greased baking dish.
5. Pour the cream mixture over the vegetables, making sure they are fully coated.
6. In a small bowl, mix together the almond flour and melted butter to make a crumbly topping.
7. Sprinkle the almond flour mixture over the top of the vegetables.
8. Bake for 20-25 minutes, or until the topping is golden brown and the vegetables are fully cooked.
9. Serve hot and enjoy!

GREEK CAULIFLOWER RICE BOWL

INGREDIENTS

1 head cauliflower, riced

1 lb ground lamb or beef

1 red onion, diced

2 cloves garlic, minced

1 cup cherry tomatoes, halved

1/2 cup kalamata olives, pitted and halved

1/4 cup crumbled feta cheese

1/4 cup chopped fresh parsley

2 tbsp olive oil

1 tsp dried oregano

Salt and pepper, to taste

DIRECTIONS

1. Heat the olive oil in a large skillet over medium heat. Add the diced red onion and minced garlic, and cook until the onion is softened and translucent.

2. Add the ground lamb or beef to the skillet, and cook until browned and fully cooked through.

3. Add the riced cauliflower to the skillet, and stir to combine. Cook for 5-7 minutes, or until the cauliflower is tender and cooked through.

4. Add the halved cherry tomatoes and halved kalamata olives to the skillet, and stir to combine. Cook for an additional 2-3 minutes, or until the tomatoes are slightly softened.

5. Season the mixture with dried oregano, salt, and pepper to taste.

6. Divide the mixture into 4 bowls, and top with crumbled feta cheese and chopped fresh parsley.

7. Serve hot and enjoy.)

Lemon Garlic Butter
Chicken with Green Beans

Ingredients

4 chicken breasts
Salt and pepper
1 tablespoon olive oil
4 tablespoons unsalted butter
4 cloves garlic, minced
1/4 cup chicken broth
Juice of 1 lemon
1/4 cup heavy cream
1 lb fresh green beans

Method

1. Preheat the oven to 400°F.
2. Season the chicken breasts with salt and pepper on both sides.
3. In a large skillet, heat the olive oil over medium-high heat. Add the chicken and cook for about 4 minutes on each side, until golden brown.
4. Transfer the skillet to the oven and bake for 10-15 minutes, or until the chicken is cooked through.
5. While the chicken is baking, prepare the sauce. In a small saucepan, melt the butter over medium heat. Add the garlic and cook for 1-2 minutes, until fragrant.
6. Stir in the chicken broth and lemon juice, and bring the mixture to a simmer. Cook for 3-4 minutes, until slightly reduced.
7. Stir in the heavy cream and continue to cook for 2-3 minutes, until the sauce has thickened.
8. In a separate pot, boil the green beans for about 5 minutes, or until they are tender. Drain the water and set aside.

Sweet apple squares

★★★★☆

With cinnamon and thyme

 2 servings 🕐 15 minutes

INGREDIENTS

100 ml milk

50 g butter

3 eggs

1 tbs cocoa

2 tsp baking soda

a pinch of salt

3 eggs

DIRECTIONS

1. Nunc nulla velit, feugiat vitae ex quis, lobortis porta leo.
2. Donec dictum lectus in ex accumsan sodales. Pellentesque habitant morbi tristique.
3. Nunc nulla velit, feugiat vitae ex quis, lobortis porta leo. Donec dictum lectus in ex. lentesque habitant morbi tristique. Nunc nulla velit, feugiat vitae ex quis, lobortis porta leo. Donec dictum lectus in ex.
4. Habitant morbi tristique.Nunc nulla velit, feugiat vitae ex quis, lobortis porta leo. Donec dictum lectu,
5. Donec dictum lectus in ex accumsan sodales. Pellentesque habitant morbi tristique.

★★★★☆

Mini apple pie

🍴 2 servings   🕐 15 minutes

INGREDIENTS

100 ml milk

50 g butter

3 eggs

1 tbs cocoa

2 tsp baking soda

a pinch of salt

3 eggs

DIRECTIONS

1. Nunc nulla velit, feugiat vitae ex quis, lobortis porta leo.
2. Donec dictum lectus in ex accumsan sodales. Pellentesque habitant morbi tristique.
3. Nunc nulla velit, feugiat vitae ex quis, lobortis porta leo. Donec dictum lectus in ex. lentesque habitant morbi tristique. Nunc nulla velit, feugiat vitae ex quis, lobortis porta leo. Donec dictum lectus in ex.
4. Habitant morbi tristique.Nunc nulla velit, feugiat vitae ex quis, lobortis porta leo. Donec dictum lectu,
5. Donec dictum lectus in ex accumsan sodales. Pellentesque habitant morbi tristique.

NOTES

Nunc nulla velit, feugiat vitae ex quis, lobortis porta leo. Donec dictum lectus in ex accumsan sodales. Pellentesque habitant morbi tristique

Cheese Pizza

Prep Time :   Cook Time :   Servings :

Lorem Ipsum dolor sit
amet, consectetur quis
adipiscing elit, sed do
incididunt ut labore et
dolore magna aliqua.
Enim ad minim veniam,
quis nostrud exertation
ullamco laboris

NOTES :
Enjoyed best when
shared.

INGREDIENTS

- 2 cups of awesome
- 1/2 tsp of fun
- 3 tbsp color
- 1 cup of kindness
- salt and pepper to taste

PROCEDURE

1. Mix awesome and fun
   together.
2. Add a dash of color.
3. Flavor everything with
   kindness!

Pumpkin soup

2 servings · 15 minutes

INGREDIENTS

100 ml milk
50 g butter
3 eggs
1 tbs cocoa
2 tsp baking soda
a pinch of salt
3 eggs

NOTES

Nunc nulla velit, feugiat vitae ex quis, lobortis porta leo. Donec dictum lectus in ex accumsan sodales. Pellentesque habitant morbi tristique.

DIRECTIONS

1. Nunc nulla velit, feugiat vitae ex quis, lobortis porta leo.
2. Donec dictum lectus in ex accumsan sodales. Pellentesque habitant morbi tristique.
3. Nunc nulla velit, feugiat vitae ex quis, lobortis porta leo. Donec dictum lectus in ex. lentesque habitant morbi tristique. Nunc nulla velit, feugiat vitae ex quis, lobortis porta leo. Donec dictum lectus in ex.
4. Habitant morbi tristique.Nunc nulla velit, feugiat vitae ex quis, lobortis porta leo. Donec dictum lectu,
5. Donec dictum lectus in ex accumsan sodales. Pellentesque habitant morbi tristique.
6. Nunc nulla velit, feugiat vitae ex quis, lobortis porta leo. Donec dictum lectus in ex. lobortis porta leo.

As we come to the end of "Delicious HEALTHY FOOD -69 EASY LOW-CARB MEALS," we want to thank you for joining us on this journey towards better health and wellness. We hope that the recipes and tips in this book have inspired you to make positive changes to your diet and lifestyle, and that you've enjoyed discovering new flavors and ingredients along the way.

Remember, healthy eating is not just about restriction or deprivation, but about nourishing your body with the nutrients it needs to function at its best. By choosing nutrient-dense foods and preparing delicious and satisfying meals, you can enjoy the benefits of a healthy diet without sacrificing flavor or enjoyment.

We encourage you to continue exploring new recipes and ingredients, and to make healthy eating a lifelong habit. With dedication and consistency, you can achieve your health and wellness goals and live the life you deserve.

Once again, thank you for choosing "Delicious HEALTHY FOOD -69 EASY LOW-CARB MEALS" as your guide to healthy eating. We wish you all the best on your journey towards better health and wellness, and we look forward to seeing the positive changes that you will make in your life.

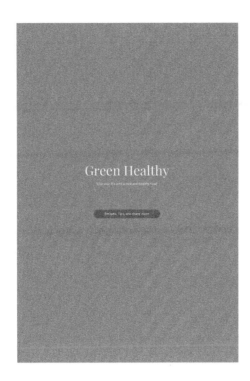

Printed in Great Britain
by Amazon

24092733R00046